IF YOU ONLY KNEW

IF YOU ONLY KNEW

PABLO PIZARRO

THE VALIENTE GROUP
PUBLISHING

Printed in the United States of America.

ISBN-13:
979-8-9897655-0-8 Paperback
979-8-9897655-1-5 Hardcover
979-8-9897655-2-2 eBook
LCCN: 2023924076

Typeset by Michelle Cline

The Valiente Group Publishing
North Arlington, New Jersey

TABLE OF CONTENTS

◆

Dedication vii

Preface ix

Introduction xiii

Chapter 1 1

Chapter 2 7

Chapter 3 13

Chapter 4 21

Chapter 5 27

Chapter 6 37

Chapter 7 45

Answered Prayers 52

Chapter 8 53

Chapter 9 61

Chapter 10 69

Chapter 11 75

Chapter 12 83

Chapter 13 91

Chapter 14 99

Marcos Rodriguez 104

Becoming Pastor Pablo 107

Chapter 15 109

Chapter 16 115

Chapter 17 123

DEDICATION

◆◆◆

To the love of my life, the woman of my youth, "my chocolate thunder," none other than my wife Erika Pizarro. Thank you for being my inspiration and for continually reminding me to finish this book. Your support and encouragement have meant the world to me. I am grateful for your prayers and for believing in the day this book would be published.

I also dedicate this book to the two most precious gifts a man could ever ask for, my daughter Savannah Pizarro and my son Zack Pizarro. Thank you for always standing by my side and believing in me. Your unwavering support has fueled my determination to see this book through to the end.

Lastly, I dedicate this book to the memory of my mentor and spiritual father, Rev. Carmelo Roman, who inspired the theme of this book. I wish you were here to read the finished story. I promise to carry out your legacy and honor the wisdom and guidance you imparted upon me.

PREFACE

◆

For quite a while, I had the idea of sharing my testimony in some form, either through writing or a recorded video. However, I kept procrastinating and putting off sharing my personal story of restoration and victory with a wider audience. While I did share what God had done in my life, it was not on a larger platform like a book or video testimony.

One day, while sitting in the congregation of the church I pastored, Lighthouse Assembly of God in Newark, New Jersey, my mentor and spiritual father, who happened to be the invited speaker that day, preached a powerful message. He passionately proclaimed, "If you only knew!" He shared how God had brought him out of difficult circumstances and expressed his passion for God. He said that if people only knew what had happened in his life, they would join him in saying, "Look at what the Lord has done."

My pastor, Rev. Carmelo Roman, went on a Holy Ghost-inspired rant, filled with fire and shouting. He shared personal stories of triumph, such as coming out of the projects, his father abandoning their family, and his joy in adopting children. Each time he exclaimed, "If you only knew," I felt a deep resonance within me. It was as if I was being prepared to receive that word and make it my own.

I remember thinking, "This is why I love being around my pastor. We share the same passion and similar testimonies." He was right. If people only knew! Not everyone is aware of what God has done in me and what He wants to do through me. Unless I share my story, the personal struggles my mother, father, sister, and brother went through will remain unknown to those who walk through the doors of our church or come in contact with me.

I should have known this after all these years. As a pastor, I preach about it: "And if someone asks about your Christian hope, always be ready to explain it" (1 Pet. 3:15 NLT).

How will they know if I don't tell everyone I come in contact with? It was in that moment, sitting in the pews of the church I pastored, that the Lord spoke to my spirit. He said, "If people only knew where I brought you out, they would have the hope and passion that you have. It's time to share your story. "This book is not meant to be like any other book. In fact, it is designed to be a sort of autobiography, sharing the stories of what God Almighty has done through His working and saving grace in my family and me. My prayer and earnest desire is to give you a glimpse inside my past and present life. As you read the words penned on these pages, I hope you begin to see how God hears the prayers of anyone who calls upon His name. It doesn't matter what age, color, or gender you are. God will hear you wherever you are, just as He heard me when I was only eight years old, sitting in a small church.

At that young age, I was a troubled kid, burdened with emotions and experiences far beyond my years. I was afraid, angry, embarrassed, and ashamed. My heart was overwhelmed and dark, which is a heavy burden for a child to bear. I felt abandoned and ignored, so much so that I was on the verge of being sent to a foster home. I often wondered why my parents lived such a difficult life filled with drugs, alcohol, and violence. Little did I know that God had an ultimate plan for my life and the lives of my family members.

My intention in writing this book is to share God's plan of transformation and change. It is for any praying mother for her wayward and backsliding child, the wife who feels helpless in the face of her abusive husband, and the husband who feels lost and clueless about how to be a father or husband. This book is for every child, youth, or young adult who feels there is no light at the end of the tunnel for them or their families.

You don't have to suffer in silence. If only you knew that God can hear your prayers and pleas.

INTRODUCTION

THE PRAYER OF AN EIGHT-YEAR-OLD BOY

I heard my grandmother tell her home health aide one morning, "I am going to call BCW," which is the Bureau of Children's Welfare, now known as Administration for Children Services, in NYC. "I know they're my grandchildren, but I just can't do it." What does a sick grandmother caring for three young children do when she's limited in resources, living in the projects, and has no one else to assist her?

I believe my grandmother, Carmen Daisy Bonilla, was a caring grandmother. My mother and father decided to drop us off at her house one day and simply disappear in search of their own vices and addictions, and she was left to take care of my brother, who had special needs, my sister, who was a girl and needed a mom and had her own needs, and not to mention me, who gave her the hardest time due to my attitude and strong will (I must admit). I don't think my grandmother was expecting to do motherhood all over again. After all, all her children were out of the house and in their late thirties.

There was my mom and my three uncles, who were all drug addicts. Something went wrong in this family. So, what could you expect from my grandmother? Every day, she cooked for us, got us ready for school, and somehow tried to keep us safe. However, the time had come that she couldn't bear it anymore.

That evening, after making dinner, she picked up the yellow old-school rotary phone and made the call. According to her, the Bureau of Children's Welfare had arranged to pick us up the next day. She said that we would go to church that night and that we should have our belongings ready so that when they came and interviewed us, we were ready to go. I was sad and frightened at the same time.

The church van came and picked us up to go to church, and my grandmother sent us off. She stayed home. Our church was located on Gleason Ave. in the Bronx. This small church believed in the power of prayer. The pastor of the church was Rev. Raul Garcia, and he was conducting a prayer service of ten to fifteen people. Before dismissing the prayer service, he asked if anyone in attendance had a personal prayer request. I was one of those kids who said everything that was going on in the house. I innocently raised my hand, and with all the emotions I felt about going to a foster home and possibly being separated from my siblings and family, I stood up and said, "I don't want to go to a foster home. If God is real, all I want is for Him to heal my mother and father and allow me to have a family. If He does, I'll tell the world about who God is."

I heard the older ladies say, "Aww, poor thing," as they gathered around my siblings and me and started to pray about what I had just said. The service was dismissed, we loaded up in the church van, and the church driver walked my siblings and me into the elevator. When we knocked on the door, our grandmother opened it with watery eyes and called us in. She hugged my sister and said, "I canceled the BCW appointment. You guys are my grandkids, and as long as I have life, I'm going to take care of you guys. I don't know how, but I will."

I just stood shocked and was like, "Wow, prayer really does work." I felt like a kid who made a magic wish, and it had just come true. But this was more than a magic wish; this was the power of an answered prayer. I was only eight years old, but God heard the cry of an eight-year-old boy who didn't even know what he was praying about—but God Almighty knew!

◆◆◆

That moment changed my life forever. I preach this every time I can. I live by the phrase: *prayer works*. The rest of my story isn't easy, but this is one of the many prayers God would answer in my life. To this present day, I'm keeping my end of the bargain with God, which is part of why I'm writing this book. I promised to tell the world who He is. If you only knew what I went through, you'd understand why I talk about Him everywhere I go.

IF YOU ONLY KNEW THEIR PAST

If you only knew the kids were watching—the parties, the fights, the drugs, and alcohol—Dad and Mom and uncles with the syringes as I would look through the bottom crease of the bathroom door. I would make a lot of money collecting the cans and bottles from leftover parties.

The beatdowns my mother would get—fork to the ear, broken leg, shattered bone right through the middle of her leg—domestic violence was alive and well in my house. The struggle was real. We would hide behind doors. My father was the "super" (superintendent), so everyone came looking for him. His brothers saw him like a hero, but he was so violent.

CHAPTER 1

◆

MY FATHER

In the early seventies, my father was a Golden Gloves featherweight boxer who derived from Santurce in San Juan, Puerto Rico, on a tour to the United States in hopes of a large prize fight and fame. He would travel through New York and meet new people, soon forgetting about boxing.

If you're not familiar with life in the seventies in New York, let me get you acquainted. They called it the Summer of Sam, as a serial killer had gone on a mad killing spree. The Bronx (where my father landed) was said to be burning. The abandoned buildings you see today in Detroit are nothing compared to what New York had going on. It was part of a culture called "The Free Love" era; polyester shirts, bell bottoms, and sideburns were the common trend. New York City was the largest urban area in the US, with a population of 7.9 million. Coming to this big metropolis opened up the eyes of a young aspiring boxer.

My dad never had a relationship with his family. His mother died due to postpartum depression. His dad soon formed a new family with another woman. This woman had other children, and along with his children from his deceased wife, they formed the "Brady Bunch." I had always been confused as to why half my aunts and uncles were of light complexion was nice eyes and good hair while the other half were dark with not-so-good hair. My father's dad would soon leave Puerto Rico, along with his newly formed family, except for one—he left my dad behind. He left him to fend for himself.

Boxing became an escape for my dad. He turned to violent actions toward others. He resented his dad for being left behind. Soon, boxing would provide him with the ticket to leave the island of Puerto Rico, only to find a whole other world in the great USA. He landed in NYC in the mid-seventies. While he was running the streets of NYC, and once he reunited with his brothers and stepbrother (the light and not-so-light-skinned ones), it seems like he went on a mission to try and prove that he was big and bad enough to defend himself and that he was the "warrior of the family." He became the one all my uncles would call if there was a "beef." The streets knew that Pablo was a big bad dude.

In the mid to late seventies, he met my mom, Noemi Bonilla. Now, my mom had a rough upbringing of her own. Her story is one that just makes you say, "Wow."

WHY WAS I BORN INTO THIS FAMILY?

Have you ever wondered, "How did I end up in this family?" That's exactly how I felt. My mother was struggling with addiction, and my father was battling alcoholism and abusive behavior toward women. Many of my parents' relatives were also caught up in substance abuse. Consequently, my siblings were born with special needs due to the drug use. I felt completely left out and even ashamed of my family background.

Have you ever looked at your friends or neighbors and thought they had a perfect family with no problems? Well, let me tell you, that's not entirely the case. Every family has its own struggles, and every person has their own flaws. As the Bible says, "All of us have sinned and fallen short of God's glory" (Rom. 3:23 CEV). In other words, nobody is perfect.

That nice family living across the street with their fancy cars and successful careers may very well be facing challenges in their marriage. Their children might be hiding secrets like pornography or drug usage from their parents. They may not even eat together as a family at the table.

It's important to realize that God placed me in my family for a purpose. You can be that catalyst for change. You can be the voice of reason in your family and help guide them onto the right path. Have you ever considered that by seeking God and asking Him to save your family and use you to make a difference, it could actually happen?

You have the power to change the trajectory of your family's life by:

1. Pursuing education and achieving your goals, even when people doubt you,

2. Choosing to stay away from alcohol and drugs, despite the influence of friends and family,

3. Surrounding yourself with positive influences and making wise choices about the company you keep, and

4. Finding true love and committing to a lasting marriage, regardless of societal norms or family expectations.

In parting, remember that God has a message for you regarding this situation: "For I know the plans I have for you," says the Lord.

"They are plans for good and not for disaster, to give you a future and a hope"

(Jer. 29:11 NLT).

____

____

____

____

____

____

____

____

____

____

CHAPTER 2

◆

MY MOTHER

My mother was about seven or eight years of age when her father decided he would sneak into her room and molest her. He would do this continuously until my mother began to experience pains in her genital area, along with an abnormal amount of discharge. It turned out she was pregnant by her own father. When my mom came forward with this atrocity to her mother, she was ignored. My mother was at a hard moment for any little girl. Her mother refused to believe her daughter for fear of losing her husband. My grandmother ignorantly turned her eye until my mother began to show signs of neglect by way of the discharge and medical issues. You wouldn't believe it, but my grandfather only received about one year or two with probation.

My mother was sent away to a foster home until she would turn eighteen years of age. Upon being released from her foster home, she met a Marine, and they would soon get married. As told by my mother, he would go away on tour with the Marines, never to come back to her. The marriage was annulled, and she would soon take to the streets of the Bronx, New York. She started by smelling glue in school (this was addictive back in the days). Later, she would use

marijuana and escalate to heroin.

Through mutual friends, she was introduced to my dad, and they soon began dating and became a couple. My mom and dad never married; they cohabited for more than eighteen years. Those years were filled with domestic violence, drugs, and alcohol. Nothing but turmoil filled our house.

My mother miscarried at least thirteen babies. Some speculated that it may have been because of her early pregnancy and the damage that her father may have caused when he raped her at a young age. I tend to believe that it could have been a mixture of her rampant life of drugs, the beatings my dad would give her while she was pregnant, and, yes, the damage her father caused her.

I personally witnessed my dad use his great boxing skills a few times. No, he never sat with me to show me the one-two combos or uppercuts. I would see him beat my mother with those fists as if she was a man. I once saw him beat someone very badly just because he whistled at my mother.

I recall how out of control my dad was and how his actions were totally negligent. As mentioned earlier, my dad was a "super" of a large apartment building on 161st St. and McClellan Ave. Yes, right across from Yankee Stadium. He once walked into what we call a bodega (corner store) with me on top of his shoulders, both legs wrapped around his shoulders, and put his hands inside his trench coat, poking them out as if he had a gun (which he didn't). He said very loudly with his broken accent, "Dis is a steek-up! Geeve me all da moneey o I keel chu!" I saw the fear head-on in the eyes of that store clerk. He quickly gave my dad the money, and my dad walked out with me on his shoulders like nothing ever happened. I may have been about five or six years old.

He asked me, "¿*Ta bien, papi?*" (You okay, buddy?) Then, he said a remark he would always say, "Was cooking in dee pot?" I would repeat it right back with a smile every time he would say, "Was cooking in dee pot?"

Fathers are supposed to take their sons to the park and play baseball, toss a football, and tussle a little bit, not hold up a bodega . . . but this was his state of mind.

A FLOWER THAT WAS NEGLECTED

When my firstborn, Savannah, entered the world, I was at a loss for how to react. The doctor announced, "It's a girl," since we had chosen not to know the gender beforehand. I was in awe! However, I found myself worrying about things like combing her hair, bathing her, and even dressing her in a way that wouldn't make her look like a boy.

In reality, I was mistaken all along. Young girls are like delicate flowers; they simply need nurturing, care, attention, and most importantly, love (even though it requires a lot of patience). By providing these things, they can blossom beautifully.

When it comes to my own mother, sadly, she was a neglected flower. Instead of receiving the care she needed, she was let down, and her hopes were crushed. She was left to grow on her own, unable to reach her full potential because her father chose to harm her, and her mother chose not to believe her.

Despite going nearly forty years without fully blossoming, I can confidently say that today, my mother is blossoming more than ever. While her earthly father failed to be the father she needed, her heavenly Father has stepped in to fill that void.

The Bible reminds us, "Even if my father and mother abandon me, the Lord will hold me close" (Ps. 27:10 NLT). To all the wonderful flowers ready to bloom, remember that God is with you. He will never leave or harm you.

In conclusion, I want to emphasize that there is a generation of beautiful flowers—our daughters, mothers, and wives—rising up. It is crucial that we do not neglect them. Let us ensure they receive the care, love, and support they deserve.

"The flowers are springing up, the season of singing birds has come, and the cooing of turtledoves fills the air"

(Song of Sol. 2:12 NLT).

CHAPTER 3

•◆•

MY BABY BROTHER: CARLOS

On June 10, 1984, my baby brother, Carlos Manuel Pizarro, was born. Up until then, I was the only boy of the family. I was used to it being just my sister and me. I really can't recall or remember my mother being pregnant with my brother. I'm not sure if it's because I was only four years of age or she was never around. She was always getting high while pregnant with my little brother. All I do recall is that one evening, my father picked my sister and me up from my grandfather's house and took us to the Bronx Lebanon Hospital. I was able to see my baby brother through a window, but all I saw were two patches on his eyes and a big light shining on his face as he lay trembling in an incubator.

I asked my dad, "What's wrong with the baby?" (I didn't even know his name yet).

My dad just told me, "He's just sick. He will be okay."

Days, weeks, and months went by, and I recall having to go visit the baby at the hospital or waiting for my father to return back from the hospital. I often wondered, *Why can't the baby come home with us?* As I grew older and gained more understanding, I came to know that my brother was born addicted to crack and cocaine. This was due to my mother's constant drug abuse while she was pregnant with my brother. My mom would smoke crack from a pipe while pregnant with my brother Carlos. Her drug addiction was so gripping that even when she gave birth to him and he was in the hospital in an incubator, she went back to using crack.

Years later, my brother would suffer from the effects of being born addicted to crack and cocaine, so much so that he was mute until the age of seven years old. Doctors told my family that he would never be able to live a normal life, was expected to only go to the fifth or sixth grade, and would have to attend a special needs school. I remember my brother humming or making noises in order for us to communicate. I never heard him say a word.

One day while we were attending a special evangelistic service, a preacher laid hands on my brother and said he would be healed. Nothing happened then, but when we got home, to our amazement, my brother looked at me and said, "Junior, I'm hungry."

I said, "What did you say?"

And he said it again, "I'm hungry."

I ran to my sister and said, "Come here. Listen to him."

He said to her, "I'm hungry."

We ran to our grandmother and dad and told them that he was speaking. We were all amazed.

From that day, my brother spoke full sentences. He never learned how to speak with a speech therapist or speech coach. The power of God healed my brother, and he and our entire family can attest to seeing God do this unbelievable miracle in our family. (Side note: to this day, my bother does not stop speaking. Boy, can he talk! Just kidding!)

As for him never reaching past the sixth grade? Well, he not only surpassed that but actually graduated high school and went on to start college—yes, college. He's currently working on a degree in music. Yes, he sings like an opera singer . . . Praise the Lord!

◆

YOU'RE NOT A MISTAKE

Have you ever felt like you were a mistake? Perhaps you believed that you shouldn't have been born, that you were the result of a fling or a one-night stand. You may have felt like a mistake.

Many could have said the same about my younger brother, Carlos, whom we affectionately call *Chiqiting* in Spanish, meaning "tiny." We named him that because when my father brought him home from the hospital, he was so small that he could fit in the palm of one's hand, like a small pet. His size was almost unbelievable, so my father introduced him to my sister and me as "tiny."

He was unrealistically tiny because my mother and father made the unfortunate decision to abuse drugs while my brother was still in my mother's womb. As a result, he was born prematurely and what society would label a "crack baby." He had to rely on machines and was born addicted to crack.

Doctors predicted that he would face many challenges and might not even finish school due to his learning disabilities.

My own brother could have easily concluded that he was a terrible mistake of life. However, let me share something amazing with you. My brother was mute and couldn't speak until he was around seven years old, but God healed him. Despite all his special needs, he not only made it through kindergarten to high school, but he also graduated. He even attended community college!

God will never make a mistake in creating us. He takes our challenges and turns them into wonderful opportunities. That's why the Bible says, "I praise you because of the wonderful way you created me. Everything you do is marvelous! Of this, I have no doubt. Nothing about me is hidden from you! I was secretly woven together out of human sight, but with your own eyes, you saw my body being formed. Even before I was born, you had written in your book everything about me" (Ps. 139:14–16 CEV).

If my brother was considered a mistake, then please explain how:

-   He can memorize every license plate number by heart after seeing it just once.

- He can provide you with the stats of any sports team, especially his favorite teams.

- He can memorize numbers and addresses instantly.

I want to leave you with these parting words. You may be labeled as weak or a mistake due to your flaws, disabilities, and special needs. But I know a God who can take what you perceive as a mistake and transform it into a powerful gift.

Listen to what God has to say about your weakness or mistake:

"My gift of undeserved grace is all you need. My power is strongest when you are weak"

(2 Cor. 12:9 CEV).

So, if Christ keeps giving me his power, I will gladly boast about how weak I am.

____

____

____

____

CHAPTER 4

MY OLDER SISTER: BRENDA

My sister, Brenda Pizarro, is the oldest of our siblings. My sister is very special to me in many ways. To this day, every Mother's Day, I make sure I give her special praises and accolades for being the mother I didn't have. She was born on May 16, 1975, addicted to cocaine, and was also premature. Her issues would lead to her being placed in special education classes all her life. However, she didn't quite suffer as much as my baby brother did.

I always like to think that my sister has to be one of the strongest human beings I've ever met. You see, sometimes when parents love their life of drugs and alcohol, it is usually the older sibling who is left to take care of the other brothers and sisters. This was the case for my sister, Brenda. Keep in mind, she had her own learning limitations and was the only female sibling.

My mom and dad would oftentimes leave us, and it was my sister who would heat up food for us or clean after us. My brother needed special attention due to being born addicted to crack and cocaine. He was mute and really had emotional needs as well, yet Brenda did the best she could. She made sure to change his diaper, potty train him, bathe him, and cook for us. She

would wake us up in the morning and serve us breakfast. Of course, this would affect my sister's education, causing her sometimes to miss school because my parents weren't around and she had to take care us. I remember how truancy officers would come and check in on us and how my sister always managed to keep her composure.

My sister has always been on God's radar. To this day, she's had her challenges because of how we were raised; however, Brenda managed to finish high school. She wasn't supposed to make it being in special ed, but she went on to study culinary arts. Yes, she loves to cook.

Quite frankly, I thought she would never want to get married and have her own kids, but God has been good to her, and today she has a child of her own and has been married for well over eleven years. She still has her challenges, but one thing that has not changed is her hard work ethic. She never complains. God has given her a peaceful spirit.

I love you, Brenda. Thank you for being our mom when we didn't have one.

◆◆◆

FORCED TO BE A LEADER

If you ever sit down and watch TV late in the evenings, you will often come across a thirty-minute segment highlighting the plight of poor countries and the need for donations to help families and abandoned children. I've seen segments where little children have lost their parents due to tragic circumstances, leaving the oldest child to assume the role of family leader.

While my family may not have experienced such a devastating loss, crack, cocaine, and alcohol certainly had a destructive impact on my parents. They would disappear for weeks, if not months, leaving us three children abandoned and unsupervised. You see, when parents prioritize their life of drugs and alcohol, it is often the older sibling who takes on the responsibility of caring for the younger ones. In my family, that was my sister, Brenda.

Brenda herself was born prematurely and addicted to drugs. However, I have never encountered a more patient, loving, and calm person like her. She assumed the role of a leader from day one.

When our parents were absent, Brenda would:

- Feed us,
- Change my brother's diapers,
- Care for our special needs baby brother,
- Wash our clothes, and so much more.

She loved my brother and me like a mother.

As we grew into adults, Brenda would often say that she never wanted to have children of her own, and she held onto that belief for a while until she had my one and only nephew. However, I had no doubt that she would love him just as she loved us.

God's Word says, "Don't be afraid. I am with you. Don't tremble with fear. I am your God. I will make you strong, as I protect you with my arm and give you victories" (Isa. 41:10 CEV). Indeed, He protected us through our sister and her love and kindness.

I leave you with these parting words: Sometimes, we are thrust into leadership not by our own choosing but because someone else depends on us. This is actually God's will. You possess all the qualities necessary to be a leader.

"Always be gentle with others"

(Phil. 4:5 CEV).

*"Give thanks in all circumstances; for this is God's
will for you in Christ Jesus"*

(1 Thess. 5:18 NIV).

CHAPTER 5

•◆•

NIGHTMARES IN MY GRANDMOTHER'S HOUSE

Usually, when little children can't sleep or are tormented by nightmares and boogie monsters, they run to their parents' bedroom and tuck themselves right in between Mommy and Daddy! I can't recall when I was able to do that!

I remember when my mother and father went missing for about three years, I would wonder if I would ever see my parents again. My grandmother thought my parents were both dead. My mother's mom was left to care for us. My older sister and younger brother would sleep with my grandmother, and I was left to sleep in the living room. This was in the Bronx River projects. I'll never forget it, 1472 Bronx River Ave Apt 4F.

Life was filled with a cranky seventy-plus-year-old non-affectionate grandmother. She was tough . . . I know she meant well, and of course, she loved us, but sheesh, she was militant. If she didn't have her coffee with Stella D'oro

Anisette cookies and couldn't gossip with her home attendant early in the morning, her day was miserable.

She always had lunch by 12 p.m., which consisted of soda crackers, potted meat, and *jugo de parcha* (passion fruit juice). Yes, that was lunch almost every day. At night, dinner would vary, but it was usually pork chops, corned beef with potatoes, or an egg with white rice. It depended on what time in the month it was. If it was the first of the month, we were good!

About 7 p.m., after dinner, my grandmother would take off to her room, along with my sister and little brother, and watch *las novelas* (Spanish soap operas). I would be left in the living room because I think I had ADHD, and I would not let her enjoy her *novelas*. From 7–10 p.m., it was soap operas. I was left to play with my baseball cards and watch the New York Yankees on a black-and-white TV (mind you, it was the nineties, not the sixties) while my grandmother had the nice color TV in her room. I recall hearing Phil Rizzuto, Tom Seaver, and Bobby Murcer call games on WPIX 11. I dreaded when the game was over because usually around 10 p.m. or 11 p.m., it was time to sleep. I never wanted to go to sleep.

I was alone every single evening from 7–10pm, but when bedtime came, I was so afraid because the apartment next door had an old lady named Mrs. Jones, and she would lock her son out of the apartment because he was a crack addict. I can recall like it was yesterday. I would be sound asleep, and he would bang on the door from 12 a.m. or 1 a.m. until sometimes sunrise . . . All I would hear was *bang, bang, bang!* "Let me in, Momma! Let me in. I'ma kill you. I'm telling you, I'ma kill you!"

He once kicked the door in, broke her guarded chain, and began beating on poor old Mrs. Jones. I heard that poor lady screaming, taking beating after beating, and all I could do was remain on the sofa bed, shivering from fear and covered with my blanket over my head. If I tried going to my grandmother's room, I would hear it or get it!

I can remember the tears flowing down my eyes some nights. I also remember having to wake up early to catch the yellow school bus, and some mornings, I was just too tired since I had just fallen asleep around 3 a.m. I would wake up some mornings and have to walk into the

hallway by myself, and there on the hallway floor was Mrs. Jones's son, lying down and sleeping in front of his mother's door. I was terrified just trying to tippy-toe right over him and get to the elevator.

Those were nights I would never ever forget. I didn't have my mom or dad to cuddle with or tell them what was going on. I call these days nightmares in my grandmother's house! I can still remember her yellow plastic-covered sofas (they were very sticky to sleep on), the lamps I would eventually break on each side of the sofas, and the big old black-and-white TV. I would have given anything for my parents to hold me on those nights.

Those mornings I got up so tired and had to be in school all day, and after taking the yellow bus to and from school, took a toll on me. My behavior on the bus or in school was poor. I would fight with other students. I never bullied anyone, but I always had a defensive stance. If someone wanted to approach me, I was always on edge.

I would go home after school to watch *Double Dare* on channel five, *Where in the World Is Carmen Sandiego?*, or *Video Music Box*. I just wanted to relax, but my grandmother was grumpy, so I was edgy at home and began to misbehave and yell back at her. Things were getting bad!

I would yell aloud, "I want my dad! He's going to beat you up when he finds out how you treat me!"

She would say, "Your dad and your mom are losers. They don't care about you. Don't even bring them up!"

I would cry intensely and dread that 7 p.m. would come, as it would start all over again—my brother and sister would leave to the bedroom with Abuela, and I would be left alone.

Then, there was my uncle (my mother's older brother). I'll refrain from using his name. I can vividly remember that in the projects where we lived, there was a lot of commotion and police activity. In those days, there were NYC housing police and regular NYC police officers. There were a lot of police and even a helicopter flying over our tall housing project. Little did I know, there was a massive police hunt for my uncle. They came knocking on our door, but not

just knocking, almost breaking it down. You wouldn't guess who was sleeping on the yellow couch next to the door? Yes, me! All I heard was, "This is the police! Open up. We have a warrant for the arrest of (my uncle's name)."

My uncle happened to have been staying there, and they busted that door down and took him. It was a scene that a boy at the age of seven should not have seen. It seems as if my uncle was wanted for escaping from prison. Apparently, he was hiding out at my grandmother's house. He was transported back to prison, and I wouldn't see him probably for another six years or so.

My grandmother sure dealt with a lot. I don't blame her crankiness. As I look back now, I feel really terrible all her children were hooked on drugs and in jail. My mother had two older brothers and a younger brother, herself being the only girl. All of them turned to a long life of drugs and crime. As I write this book, one of them is nearly in his sixties and still in jail. To me, these experiences were what I call nightmares at my grandmother's house.

•◆•

HOUSE OF HORRORS

Have you ever watched horror movies? Although I don't recommend them, these movies often revolve around a villain or monster who seeks to kill and destroy people. They are filled with madness and screaming.

Growing up in my grandmother's apartment in the projects, it felt like living in a house of horrors. I was constantly filled with panic and nervousness because some very dangerous individuals occupied the building. To make matters worse, there was chaos within my own apartment:

- We didn't eat meals together.
- There was constant arguing and bickering.
- I could hear my neighbors fighting.

It truly was a house of horrors.

What should a household feel like? God's Word says, "In your house, your wife will be like a vine full of fruit. All around your table, your children will be like olive trees, freshly planted. That's how it goes for anyone who honors the LORD: they will be blessed!" (Ps. 128:3–4 CEB).

The image portrayed here is that when we honor God in our home:

- The wife/mother will be fruitful.
- Children will gather at the table for nourishment, providing an opportunity for quality time and understanding their needs, worries, and development.
- By doing these things, we prepare our children for adult life, planting them correctly.

I understand that I grew up in a house of horrors, and you may have had a similar experience. However, this doesn't mean that we cannot experience the beautiful image depicted in Psalm 128. We can start by honoring God. While the devil comes to bring destruction, the Lord has come to give us life— life in our homes, marriages, communities, and wherever we go.

I leave you with these parting words: If you want to escape your house of horrors, there's only one thing to do: have faith in the Lord Jesus, and you will be saved! This applies to everyone who lives in your home (Acts 16:31 CEV).

CHAPTER 6

•◆•

MY FATHER'S ARREST

One afternoon, I was at a pizza shop in the Soundview section of the Bronx on Morrison Ave. I recall playing a video arcade game and seeing everyone in the pizza shop run out and shout, "Wow! Ooh!" They were shouting and reacting to a group of undercover narcotics police officers arresting and taking my father to the ground. It seems like my dad had been "resisting" because they were beating him pretty good.

What's a young boy to do when he witnesses his dad being aggressively arrested? Is a young boy expected to be exposed to this? I saw how he was roughed up, bruised, and beaten, then taken away in handcuffs and placed inside the paddy wagon. After that day, I probably didn't see my dad for about two to three years. He was arrested for possession of narcotics with the intent to sell or distribute.

My mom and dad were known drug addicts but were also known as drug dealers; they would make money by selling drugs on the corner of Morrison Ave. and Westchester Ave.

Now, with my father being incarcerated, it was just my mother in the streets alone, selling drugs and getting high while my older sister Brenda and younger brother Carlos were alone with my grandma just a few miles away in the projects of Bronx River Ave.

While my dad was in prison and my siblings and I were living with my grandmother, my mother was running wild on the streets. I always had her on my mind. I feared that something bad would happen to her. I would go to school worried and question if she was okay. I would stay up late, hoping she would just come home to my grandmother's house, but she wouldn't.

I remember on the weekends walking from 174th Street and Bronx River Ave. all the way to Morrison and Soundview just to see if my mom was okay. I had to be about eleven or twelve years old. I would look all over for her, and when I found her, I would act like the adult. I would scream at her and say, "Mom, let's go home! Please don't stay here! I'm worried for you!" My mother was so addicted to crack she just did not care. She was in terrible shape. She had abscesses on her arms, chapped lips, and black eyes. It was a horrific way to see your mother.

My heart couldn't take seeing her like that, so much so that on one weekend, I never returned to my grandmother's house. I stayed with my mom and literally lived and stayed with her on the streets for weeks. Yes, I didn't go back to school. I was truant for most of my fourth grade. Let that sink in . . . fourth grade! I would stay wherever my mother stood. I would watch her go into parks and other people's cars and light up crack pipes, inject needles, and drink. I was literally her shadow. I wouldn't leave her sight. I saw things I had no business seeing.

When my mom would sell drugs, there were times when she would have me hold them so that if the police would come, they would never find them on her. I witnessed her deal the blue, red, and yellow tops (crack vials). I saw her cook the crack, prepare the bags, and fill the vials. I knew what the code names were for when cops were around and they wanted to signal it to the other drug runners—phrases and sayings like "5-0" (I guess from the detective show *Hawaii Five-0*), and Spanish terms like "*va bajando*" (they're coming down). Instead of being in a classroom getting an education, I was on the streets receiving a ghetto orientation. The streets were raising me.

If a normal child wants a gift, he simply asks his parents. In my case, if I wanted a Nintendo Gameboy, I would ask my mother, and she would say, "Give me an hour or two. Let me sell this stash or see if someone comes around with a Gameboy they stole, and I will get it for you." Oftentimes, my mother would always come through and buy me chains, sneakers, and Nintendo Gameboys right from the streets. You might ask yourself, is this something a young child who hasn't reached his preteen years yet should live and learn? I believe my mom would do these things so that I would leave her alone or not shadow her so much.

DEVOTIONAL

•◆•

LIFE PUSHES YOU HARD

Sometimes life can be rough and brutal. I compare life to a bully who constantly pushes you around until you've had enough.

Have you ever felt like life hasn't been kind to you? Some common experiences include:

- The untimely or unexpected death of a loved one

- Betrayal by those you loved the most

- A series of bad experiences where it feels like you just can't catch a break

I understand that feeling. I, too, wanted to be a normal kid, playing football and coming home to a smiling mom after school. Instead, I witnessed my father's arrest, my mother being abused, and my siblings facing setbacks due to our parents' drug use. Life was pushing us around and beating us down like two black eyes and broken ribs until we had enough.

Here's what God's Word says: *"I was pushed back and about to fall, but the Lord helped me. The Lord is my strength and my defense; he has become my salvation"* (Ps. 118:13–14 NIV).

Just because life keeps pushing us and treating us like a punching bag, it doesn't mean we have to lie down and take it. We have to reach a point where we get tired of living that way. There is hope, and there is light at the end of the tunnel. My family and I were pushed hard, but the Lord helped us and defended us.

I leave you with these parting words: *"The LORD supports all who fall down, straightens up all who are bent low"* (Ps. 145:14 CEB).

You don't have to stay low on the floor. There's someone waiting for you with a stretched-out hand. Your family can overcome this! Don't let life continue to push you around. Get up and rise above it!

____

____

____

CHAPTER 7

•◆•

MOM BEING DRAGGED

One evening, on the very same street my father was arrested a few years prior, I saw what seemed to be a riot. Bottles were flying, and garbage cans lit on fire were being thrown at a car; rocks, bats, you name it, and it was used to stop a blue midsize car. Why were people rioting against this car? This car was literally dragging my mother, who was hanging from the driver's side. My mom was being dragged at least one hundred feet. She was screaming. Everyone was yelling, and I was running behind the car just trying to catch up to see what was going on.

Eventually, the car sped off, and she remained in the middle of the street with major burns on her legs, arms, and side of her face. I was mortified, upset, and angry. At that age, I shouldn't have been exposed to that. The feelings I had were not supposed to be experienced by a young child my age. Luckily, she survived that!

You might ask, why was she dragged by a car? Well, there's a song by a well-known rapper who is now dead called The Notorious B.I.G. or Biggie Smalls. That song was called "Ten Crack Commandments," and one of the commandments in that song went a little something

like this: "Never get high on your own supply." My mother did just that. She took a known drug dealer's crack, and instead of selling it, she smoked it all up. When it came time to surrender the money from her day of selling drugs, she had none. I guess that did not make some people happy, and that's why she was dragged. My mom had to hide out for a while because they were looking for her.

There was another time when she had gone into a store, and one of the drug dealers she owed money to followed her into the bodega. He pushed her up against a refrigerator and began to punch her several times like a man. I was right behind her. I opened a refrigerator door, took out a Snapple bottle, shattered it, and held on to the knob or top portion, acting as if I was going to cut the guy. I did this to distract him so my mom could run out the store. This man took that bottle from me and attempted to slash my face, but I quickly put my left hand up, and he sliced my wrist open. He then facepalmed me and smashed my head right into a glass refrigerator, splitting the back of my head open. My mom got away, and the store owners got the guy off me and out the store. All I can remember was being taken in an ambulance and then in the hospital meeting my mom.

I received fourteen stitches in my left wrist and some butterfly stitches in my head. Until this day, I look at both scars, and I'm reminded of God's divine covering. My face should've been scarred, and my head should've been split open further, but God had his hand on me. Today, when I get a haircut, you can clearly see the scar on my head, but it reminds me how I took the hits for my momma.

•◆•

DRAGGED THROUGH THE MUD

There's an old saying that goes, "I'm being dragged through the mud." This saying implies that when someone drags you through the mud, they are spreading negative rumors and attempting to tarnish your reputation. Unfortunately, this was the reality in my life and that of my family. Every time I went to school, I had to endure ridicule and taunting because my mother's reputation was *being dragged through the mud*. Let's be honest, she played a significant role in it, as her reputation as a drug addict and fiend was well-known. I had to deal with comments like, "Isn't your mother the lady in the corner begging for money?" or "Your mother was seen doing questionable things." These situations caused me to get into fights at school as I tried to defend her honor and reputation.

In addition to being figuratively dragged through the mud, my mother was physically dragged many feet from a car because of her association with dangerous individuals. This incident became the talk of the town, and people would look at me and shake their heads, probably out of pity.

This is what the devil does to us; he drags us through the mud. His desire is to ruin our lives, happiness, and reputation. However, God's Word says, *"He restores my soul; He leads me in the paths of righteousness for His name's sake"* (Ps. 23:3 NKJV).

When we fully surrender ourselves to God and serve Him, He not only restores our name and past actions, but He also restores our souls and sets our lives on a completely new path. He does this so that His name may be glorified, taking all the credit.

God has restored my mother to such an extent that if you were to look at her today, you would never believe she was once involved with hard drugs and dragged through the mud. She is still talked about in town, but now it's because of the love she has for God, her children, and her grandchildren. You should see how well she spoils my kids. Some people will never know God restored her reputation.

I leave you with these parting words: *"You intended to harm me, but God intended it for good to accomplish what is now being done, the saving of many lives"* (Gen. 50:20 NIV).

Don't allow yourself to be dragged through the mud. Don't let stains from the past and a bad reputation hinder you from living out your future and fulfilling your purpose.

ANSWERED PRAYERS

CHAPTER 8

•◆•

FATHER'S RELEASE FROM JAIL

After not attending school for several months and almost missing the entire fourth grade simply because I wanted to be around my mother, the time had come to go back to my grandmother's house. Somehow, the truancy office made sure that I would go back and that my grandmother would have guardianship over me.

When I returned to the Bronx River projects, I would go without seeing my mother for several years. Remember, my father was incarcerated, and now my mom was on the streets of NYC, not thinking about her children. My grandmother tried to raise me as best as she could, but I'm sure it was difficult raising two special needs children and one hyperactive child (that's me). Thankfully, she would send us to church, and I would become involved and remain active for quite some time.

It was there where I learned to pray for the condition my parents were in.

I desired a normal family. I would see most people with their mothers and fathers, yet I didn't have that. I recall several Mother's Days when the pastor of the church would ask the children to go and hug their moms and pray over them or take a flower to them, but I couldn't

experience that. There were always nice ladies or grandmothers who would come up to us and hug us. My tears would well up, and feelings of rebellion developed in me. I didn't want the pity hugs. This was an extremely hard time for my siblings and me. We craved and starved for the love of a strong and normal family.

One Christmas season, my prayers were about to be answered. Remember, I prayed in a small church several years before that if God was real, he would not let me go to a foster home and be split apart from my family. I also prayed that God would heal my mother and father from alcoholism and drugs. I said that if he would do this for me, I would tell the world about who God was. Well, the first prayer was answered. My grandmother had canceled the foster home appointment, but that was it. Both my parents were still on drugs and out of our lives. So, here we were. Dad was incarcerated for quite some time now, and my mom had not been in contact with us for a long time. My siblings and I were practically orphans. My poor grandmother was stressed and upset with my parents for basically abandoning us.

However, I remember it was around Christmas season. I was at my grandmother's house when I heard a loud knock on the door of the apartment. I, being the nosy one who always answered the door, climbed on a chair and looked through the peephole. I was shocked, totally amazed about what my eyes were seeing through the peephole. It was my dad wearing a long dark trench coat and carrying wrapped-up Christmas boxes. I jumped off that chair and yelled to my grandmother, "The door, the door; it's my dad!"

She wasn't too happy. I rushed back to the door and opened it fast, and there he was. He hugged me and kissed me and gave me a wrapped-up box. My brother and sister both came out, and while he was greeting us, my grandmother, visibly upset, said, "What are you doing here?"

He said, "I've come to see my kids. Let's not fight . . ."

She went back and forth with him for a bit. These were the words that stay with me until this day; he said to my grandmother, "I was just released from jail, and I accepted Jesus while I was in there. I've decided to turn my life around."

My grandmother contradicted him and said, "That's what everyone says when they're in jail. They all meet Jesus!"

He said, "I did, and not only that, but I'm also coming to take full custody of my children. I'm going to raise them knowing about God."

My grandmother yelled, "Yeah, right!" and slammed the door in his face.

•◆•

JUST CRY OUT

How does a newborn baby communicate? That's right, they cry. They cry when they're hungry, tired, sick, or in need of a diaper change. Children are well-known for crying, and if left unattended, it can be quite bothersome to our ears. So, what do good parents do? They attend to their children's needs to soothe their cries.

Many of us are crying out today. We cry out for love, affection, a sense of belonging, and for our families. I know this because I, too, have been crying out since I was eight years old. I cried out for loving parents, a normal family, and peace of mind. Honestly, I felt like an unattended crying baby for a long time until I discovered how to cry out to God.

God's Word says, *"I was a nobody, but I prayed, and the Lord saved me from all my troubles"* (Ps. 34:6 CEV). Other versions of this passage say, "I cried out." You see, crying out to God is another way of saying we pray to Him. When we pray to God, He is not like our earthly parents; He attends to His children quickly. Crying out to God is like setting off an alarm or a baby monitor in heaven. Heaven stops what it's doing for you and me.

I remember crying (praying) out to God, asking Him to change and save my family. I pleaded with Him to transform my father's lifestyle of drugs and prison and heal my mother of her addiction. And because I cried out, this nobody received an answered prayer.

I leave you with these parting words: Never think that you are too grown to cry out to your heavenly Father. Every time you come across the word *cry* in the Bible, it also means "pray." When you cry out, God stops and listens, just for you.

> *"But the LORD says, 'Because the poor are oppressed, because of the groans of the needy, I'm now standing up. I will provide the help they are gasping for'"*

(Ps. 12:5 CEB).

CHAPTER 9

•◆•

MY DAD'S WALK WITH THE LORD

For the next several weeks and months, my father kept showing up to the house faithfully. He would pick us up and take us to church. He was new in his walk. He even lived in a drug rehab program called Way-Out Ministries by Willis Ave. and 148th Street. He had no place to stay, but he would live in this men's rehab until he grew closer to God and began organizing life.

Stuff that sticks to me are moments like when my dad picked me up one day and took me to his church service at the rehab place. Afterward, he would take me to go and get hot bread or a snack and then head back to his little room. He would kneel down, make me kneel down with him, and he would say, "Pray whatever I pray."

As I write this, tears flow down my face because looking back now, I see that prayer always works. My dad began to pray; he said, "God, give me my family back. Help me to make right for all the wrongs I did. Look at my son here; bless him, separate him, and don't let him be anything like me. Use him; take him to the world to preach your Word." He prayed over me as I closed my eyes, and he would say, "Separate a good wife for him, and let him be a family man and a worshiper. He would pray for my brother and sister's healing and ask God to forgive him because they were suffering due to his and my mother's drug addiction.

I can firmly tell you that little by little, my father was becoming stronger and stronger in his walk with God. The "hood" (community that knew him) couldn't believe it. His family couldn't believe. He was a complete man, got his own little room, moved out of the rehab, and started working. He was always in church and stopped smoking and drinking. He wore a suit every day—even when there was no church!

Because of my dad's previous life, he was well-known in the community. He was known for all the bad things, the stick-ups, the parties, and violence. So when he changed, people would literally come to see him. He would offer prayers to those who would come and see him, and people were giving their lives to Christ. They were falling on the streets. This was a complete miracle, an answered prayer. As my father grew in his walk, he took a huge step in his life, and that was to fulfill what he had told my grandmother that night he came out of prison: getting full custody of my siblings and me in court.

CLEAN OUT THE VIRUS

Imagine you have a MacBook computer, and when you turn it on, the screen is blank or it doesn't respond to your commands. What would you do?

The obvious solution would be to take it to a computer technician who can assess the problem. Most likely, the technician would diagnose it as a virus that has damaged the operating software. The solution would be to clean out the virus and install brand-new operating software, making the computer work like new. However, this process would result in losing everything that was previously on the computer, as it would need to be wiped clean and started fresh.

This same scenario applied to my father. He was a troubled man who struggled with drugs, alcohol, and neglected his family. My dad was in and out of jail, and he subjected my mother to domestic abuse in the worst ways.

I don't believe that my father, or any of us for that matter, were designed or created to act so recklessly. We were created for greatness, but sometimes we catch a virus called sin.

What happened with my father is nothing short of remarkable. He had to go to the ultimate technician, Jesus Christ, who diagnosed him with the "virus" of sin. He needed to be completely "reprogrammed" and cleaned out.

God's Word says, *"Do not conform to the pattern of this world, but be transformed by the renewing of your mind. Then you will be able to test and approve what God's will is—his good, pleasing, and perfect will"* (Rom. 12:2 NIV). Once my father's mind was renewed and reprogrammed, he emerged from prison as a changed man.

Here are the remarkable changes my father experienced:

- He took responsibility for his past actions and accepted that Christ redeemed him.
- He gained full custody of my two siblings and me.
- He started attending church with us.
- He went from being a thief to helping the poor.
- He went from being in prison to preaching to prisoners.

This transformation is not limited to my father alone. It applies to each one of us. We don't have to remain the way we are. We can go to the ultimate technician, God, and He will wipe out our sinful behavior. God has already provided His Son, Jesus, to cleanse us from this virus.

I leave you with these parting words: *"But if we are living in the light, as God is in the light, then we have fellowship with each other, and the blood of Jesus, his Son, cleanses us from all sin"* (1 John 1:7 NLT). If we seek a relationship with God and turn to Him when we are infected with sin, He will cleanse us with the blood of Jesus.

Let's allow our minds to be renewed and transformed by God.

67

CHAPTER 10

◆

COURT DATE FOR CUSTODY

True to his word, several months later, there was a court hearing as my father went to court to fight for full custody of my siblings and me. This was the beginning of an answered prayer. My father was now clean and taking responsibility for his life and his kids.

My grandmother somehow got ahold of my mother, who had been missing for months, and told her she was going to lose her kids. She advised her to show up to court and at least try and fight for us. To our surprise, my mother did show up.

When it was time to go before the judge, my father stated that he was there to obtain full custody of his three children. My mother was there, and she argued that she was in the process of getting her life together and that her mother (my grandmother) was helping her raise the children.

Now, my dad did not know too much English. He needed a translator. So, when the judge said to him (I'm paraphrasing), "Now, you know you have a wide folder and a big criminal history. You're asking for custody of these children, and you think you're fit?"

My dad did something that was quite different. When I translated what the judge had asked him, he said, "Oh, dile a el que ese era yo. Ya no soy ese hombre, y dile que Jehová es mi pastor y nada me faltará." So, I translated back to the judge what he said (are you ready for this?), "Tell him that was me. I am no longer that man, and tell him that the Lord is my shepherd, and I shall not lack anything." Yep, Psalm 23, and with an attitude, he said it.

The judge stared, stayed quiet for a brief second, and then said, "Okay, I'm granting you full custody of your children. Be responsible and do what you have set out to do. Good luck."

I saw his face when I told him. He wasn't expecting that. You know who else's face I glanced at? My mother's because she wasn't expecting that either. She kissed us and walked out, looking pretty disappointed. After that day, it would be several years before I would see my mom again.

My father immediately started looking for an apartment. He wasn't even expecting this miracle. He was about to be a responsible father. His prayer of "God, give me my family back" was answered! I saw how my father quickly took us out of the projects and moved us into a private house. He cooked and cleaned for us. He began to teach my older sister how to cook. He learned to deal with my brother's special needs. He would take my brother to speech therapy and for special appointments. He never failed in taking us to church during the week and weekends; if there was a service, we were there. Within me, I could say that God not only answered my father's prayer of "give me my family back," but he also answered this eight-year-old boy's prayer and saved my father.

However, I had only a somewhat Christian home. There was one thing missing, and that was my mom. Many in our family thought she had died since we had not heard or seen from her in years. We would go looking for her on the block where she would normally hang out and get high, but we could not find her. My grandmother, who was now very ill, had no clue. Her brothers had no clue. Quite frankly, we thought she was dead, and it was a matter of time before we would be notified that she was killed or had overdosed.

•◆•

FIGHT YOUR OWN BATTLES

Growing up, I remember being in school and finding myself in situations where disagreements and fights would arise. In those moments, I would often seek the help of my friends to stand against those who were causing trouble for me. However, there were also times when I heard the expression, "Fight your own battles." Do you recall hearing that too?

I was frequently reminded to take responsibility for my own challenges and not rely on others to solve my problems. If I made a mess, it was my responsibility to clean it up.

When my dad made the decision to turn his life around and act responsibly, he faced a tremendous battle. He sought full custody of my two special needs siblings and me. Unfortunately, the odds were stacked against him. Throughout his life, he had been a violent aggressor, battled alcohol and drug addiction, and had a criminal record. It seemed like an impossible battle, and there was no one he could recruit to help him. It was reminiscent of those school days when I was told, "You're on your own with this one; fight your own battles."

Have you ever experienced a similar feeling? When you desperately need support and someone to stand by your side, yet it seems as if they are telling you to fight your own battles?

God's Word tells us, "The Lord will fight for you; you need only to be still" (Exod. 14:14 NIV). When everyone turned their backs on my dad, and he found himself without anyone to represent him in the courtroom as he fought for custody, God showed up as his advocate and fought his battles for him.

Here are the incredible things that unfolded:

- Despite his troubled past, he was granted full custody.

- The judge admitted that he didn't know why he believed my father had changed, but he decided to give him the benefit of the doubt.

- Even though my father had no apartment ready for us to live in and lacked financial resources, the judge declared, "You have full custody. Case closed. Battle over."

I leave you with these parting words: *"You won't even have to fight. Just take your positions and watch the Lord rescue you from your enemy. Don't be afraid. Just do as you're told. And as you march out tomorrow, the Lord will be there with you"* (2 Chron. 20:17 CEV).

The next time the odds seem insurmountable, remember to stay quiet and let God fight for you because He is the one who fights our battles.

CHAPTER 11

•◆•

THE VISIT TO PRISON

Years went by, and you would think this is a great ending. God is faithful, amen. Dad was saved, the kid grows up, and that's it. However, there's more. You see, my dad and mom never got back together, but he always showed me to keep praying for her. Now, I was in my teens, and I was upset at my mother for not being there for us most of our lives—not showing up to my school functions or graduations. However, my father continued to show me love and mercy through scriptures.

I began to preach in many local churches in the Bronx, and everyone wanted me to share my experience of how God saved my father and gave him back his family. Many were amazed and wanted me to share that story and sermon.

One day, a lady in our church named Juana who was in charge of the prison ministry thought it would be a great idea to have me be a guest speaker at a women's correctional facility in Upstate New York. I was underage, so a lot of steps had to be taken in order to get me clearance. Once everything was set up, my father and a group from the church arranged to go out that Saturday morning to visit the women's correctional facility.

I was checked in, and we began to preach and tell my story of how God saved my father and how God had healed my brother from speech impediments. I then closed out my speaking session with a call for prayer. I asked if there were any women there who needed prayer and believed that God could restore their family as he did with me, then to come up because I was going to personally pray for them.

I know this may sound too dramatic, but I promise all who read this that I am not adding or taking away from this. I'm giving it to you just like it happened. To my amazement, when I asked those women to come up for prayer, here came my mother, crying and pushing ladies out of the way. My eyes opened wide. My dad just looked at me in shock. We thought she was dead!

When she came to me with all the tears and excitement, the officers attempted to separate us, but I said, "That's my mom; that's my mom!" Everyone, including the officers and the church people who were with me, began crying and hugging. It was a surreal moment. I promise you that I could write a book about this! (Wait, I think that's where we're at.)

After that day, I had no doubt that God was real and that He had major plans in my life and the life of my family. When we left that prison, my mom and our family established communication again. She would soon come out of prison and live with us for a little bit, but only until she returned to her old ways and disappeared back to the streets and life of drugs.

DEVOTIONAL

•◆•

WHEN YOU LEAST EXPECT IT

Imagine a young child who dreams of one day receiving the toy or gaming system they have always wanted. The child has wished for it, prayed for it, and dropped subtle hints to their parents. However, it seems like none of their hints, prayers, or wishes have worked, as they have yet to receive the coveted item.

Life can be like that at times. We desire that dream vacation or that perfect family or spouse. We wish, pray, and work hard for that top promotion at work. Yet, things don't always go as planned. It can feel like our cries are falling on deaf ears and that we are being ignored. This can be incredibly frustrating, leading to a loss of confidence, trust, hope, and even faith in God.

I can assure you that I have been there. I was that child waiting and dreaming for something good to happen once and for all. I was tired of the string of negative events happening in my family. I had been praying, believing, and hoping for a miracle since I was eight. I longed for a normal family and a decent home for years, but it seemed like God was too busy or not interested in granting my request.

What I have come to understand about God and the life we live here on earth is that "God never shows up on time or late." He comes at just the right time. God's Word tells us, *"Put it in writing, because it is not yet time for it to come true. But the time is coming quickly, and what I show you will come true. It may seem slow in coming, but wait for it; it will certainly take place, and it will not be delayed"* (Hab. 2:3 GNB).

Isn't that awesome? How do you think that child who has been waiting for their dream toy or gaming system would feel once they finally receive that coveted gift? After all the wishing, praying, and subtle hints, the day has finally come for them to enjoy what they have been praying for.

When my mother walked down that aisle in the prison cafeteria, my eyes saw what I had been praying for. I was in utter shock, but I was ready to embrace and enjoy the gift that God graciously gave me—my mother giving her heart to the Lord. When I least expected it, God honored my prayers.

I leave you with these parting words: *"Wait for the Lord; be strong and take heart and wait for the Lord"* (Ps. 27:14 NIV). If He did it for me, He can do it for you too! Whatever you have been praying for will come to pass . . . when you least expect it.

CHAPTER 12

•◆•

MY COUSIN: BENJI

I'm thankful for my mother's cousin. He was more like an uncle or father figure. I believe that God really takes care of His children. I always felt like an orphan even though I really was not. I just never had those family moments that every child should have. I longed to play catch with my dad. I wanted to feel the embrace of my mom, but I didn't have that. In my life, I have experienced God's grace and have seen how He operates. There may be orphans and children whom their biological parents gave up, but the Lord provides good homes for them and parents who themselves could not have kids.

Well, I wasn't adopted, but I almost felt like it because my mother's cousin would come pick us up for Sunday school. My grandmother would call Benji (short for Benjamin) to come pick us up and take us to church. My grandmother wouldn't go to church as much by then because she was battling many illnesses. She also wanted relief from having to care for three grandchildren all day, so she would call cousin Benji and his wife Wanda.

Oh, the memories! We would go to Sunday school in the morning and watch films of *Gospel Bill* and sing along with my cousin (who directed the children's ministry). We would sing songs like "Father Abraham," "He's Got the Whole World in His Hands," and " Down by the Riverside." After an exciting Sunday school, we would go home and then return in the evening for the Sunday 6 p.m. evangelistic service.

Cousin Benji never took us back to our home. It's almost as if he was thinking, "Those kids don't want to go back home." He would take us to his home. I loved going to cousin Benji and Wanda's house. It felt like what a home should be. He had a room with a bunkbed for his daughters, and it was filled with stuffed animals. His house smelled so good; it smelled like they baked cakes there all the time. He had an awesome fish tank with fish he would let me overfeed, and we would also clean it out together. We would have Sunday meals together right before getting ready to go back to church.

Here is why I appreciate cousin Benji. He showed me what "table manners" were. He would say, "Elbows off the table." His wife Wanda was right behind him, saying, "Eat with a fork," and she would tell me to place a napkin on my lap. These moments were etched in my head and filed in my memory bank. It should've been my mom and dad teaching me how to eat

properly and display good table manners, but God always provides servants for His children.

Cousin Benji would buy me nice shirts and ties. He gave me my first Bible and took my cousin Nelson and me to my first Yankee game (in the old stadium, of course). I'll never forget the experience. Cousin Benji and Wanda took me to the game, and right there—who now is a nobody, but for me, was the greatest baseball player ever—was Oscar Azocar. Why was he the greatest? He gave me my first ever signed ball, and there was cousin Benji, saying, "Hey, congrats! You got a ball." My cousin Nelson was patting me on the back, and cousin Wanda was saying, "Way to go!" I remember who the Yanks played too; they played the Cleveland Indians.

After I received the ball, my cousin thought we'd probably had enough. He was tired, and the Yanks were losing, so he decided to leave. When we got outside and ready to go in the car, we heard a siren go off, the crowd cheer, and then the announcer say, "A homer for Hensley 'BamBam' Meulens!" I was really disappointed. Well, I fell in love with the Yankees, but I hate leaving games early.

My cousin Benji was a mentor. He taught me the Word. He displayed passion and treated me to the little things that every little boy desires in his family. I now see programs like Big Brothers Big Sisters and think that's the role my cousin modeled for me. Do you know that just recently, I reunited with good ol' cousin Benji!

Boys need men in their lives for the little things—the ball game experiences, the table manners instructions, and the awesome Bible lessons.

◆

NEXT MAN UP

In 2019, the New York Yankees, known as the MLB's best team, had an incredible year. It was a year filled with remarkable comebacks and victories. That team was truly special to watch, with every player contributing something significant. However, what made the 2019 season particularly remarkable was the fact that they broke a record. It wasn't the home run record or the most wins in a season but rather the record for the most players injured on a major league team in history. Approximately thirty Bronx Bombers found themselves on the injured reserve list, surpassing the previous record of twenty-six held by the Los Angeles Dodgers.

How did they manage to succeed? How did the Yankees have one of their most exciting seasons in history despite the injuries? Their manager, Aaron Boone, attributed it to the "Next Man Up" mentality. Whenever a major superstar got injured, an unknown player from the minor leagues would step in and contribute, seamlessly filling the gap left by the high-priced superstar. This happened thirty times throughout the season, and each time, the next man up kept the team going.

In my own life, the person who was supposed to be the superstar figure (my dad) was not always there for me. However, God always called upon the "Next Man Up" to help me achieve the victories I needed. I experienced success when my cousin Benji, and his wife Wanda introduced me to table manners, etiquette, and the importance of family values like having dinner together.

Although my physical father may not have shown me many of these things, it was as if the coach in heaven was looking down on me and saying, "You will succeed, my son. I'm calling upon the Next Man Up to help you." I truly believe in what God's Word says: *A father of the fatherless, a defender of widows, is God in heaven*" (Ps. 68:5 NKJV).

You may currently be a single mom, a single dad, a child seeking answers as to why your parents gave you up for adoption, or a widowed or divorced spouse searching for meaning in life, wondering why there have been so many losses. Trust and hope in the Lord, for He has the final say.

I leave you with these parting words: *"Be strong! Be fearless! Don't be afraid or scared of your enemies, because the*

LORD your God marches with you. He won't let you down, and He won't abandon you" (Deut. 31:6 CEB).

God will always empower you to stand tall and achieve victory because of the Next Man Up!

CHAPTER 13

•◆•

EMILIO NIEVES

My father lived a very rough life; he had a hard past. As you have already read within the previous chapters of this book, my dad engaged in many illegal activities; he was an alcoholic, drug addict, was violent, and abused my mom often. God had a plan for my dad, but my dad just didn't know it. You see, the Lord sent a special agent to reach out to my family, and I'd like to think that this heavenly special agent was a messenger. His name was Emilio Nieves.

Emilio would drive by in a yellow school bus—yes, a yellow school bus. He would honk the horn at my father, who was the "super" (superintendent) of a building complex on McClellan and River Ave. (yes, next to Yankee Stadium), as Emilio would drive by in the yellow school bus, honk the horn, and say, "*Dios les bendiga*" (God bless you). My dad would simply smirk and wave, but no conversation would be had.

This man would drive by our house almost every day until one day, he asked my dad if he would like to go to church with him, and my dad said, "Okay". My dad took my siblings and me with him on this yellow bus. The church was an apartment, and they were singing Spanish coritos (fast-paced hymns). We only went once, but I remember that Emilio Nieves never stopped driving by, honking the horn, and inviting us to church.

One day, my father was so drunk, and when Emilio drove by, he said, "Take my kids. I can't go," and I remember like it was today; I got on that bus, but I was deeply sorry and concerned for my dad. It hurt me to see him so drunk. I felt pain even though I was young. Why couldn't my dad be normal like everyone else? I was thinking all this while I sat on the that yellow church bus.

As I stepped off the church bus, Emilio Nieves looked at me square in the eyes and said in Spanish: "Don't fear because God is with you, and he's got a plan for your family." He then looked at me, took his index finger, placed it on my chin, and tilted my head up in gesture, saying, "Pick your head up." When we went into the service, I sat there confused, like, how did he know I was sad or concerned for my dad?

When the church service finished, I recall Brother Emilio looking at a sports zipper jacket I had on, lowering the zipper halfway, and realizing I didn't have a T-shirt or shirt under it (I had come to church on a whim). Remember, my dad had told Emilio to take me because he was too drunk to go, so I didn't have a chance to get dressed properly. Besides, we were really poor and unattended. My parents didn't care about what we put on; they were too busy doing drugs.

Upon Emilio seeing this, he took me back home, but the very next day, he came with a black bag filled with lots of clothes. I don't know if they were new or not, but I was happy to have new clothes, and they were name brand. I'm recording this story in the pages of this book because this moment in my life marked me. I wasn't embarrassed; I was blessed and thankful.

We never went back to Brother Emilio Nieves's church after that. My father really never gave his heart to the Lord at that moment, but Emilio Nieves planted such a seed in my life that today as a pastor, I have to go on the streets in our community and give stuff away. Just ask anyone who knows about Pastor Pablo or Lighthouse Assembly, and they will tell you that I live out in the community, trying to acquire and give resources to the least and the needy.

Brother Emilio Nieves remained a faithful man and did what God calls us to do: evangelism and outreach. He faithfully drove by, honked that horn, and yelled God bless you every day. He invited us, and we attended; he generously gave and never expected in return.

Several years later after my father came to Christ and started serving the Lord, my family and I got plugged into a church called Jehovah Shalom on 174th and Boston Road, and lo and behold, Brother Emilio Nieves had transferred from that apartment church he used to go to and was a member at our church.

God knows how to orchestrate everything. The seed he had planted was there for him to see bear fruit. I cry every time I think of Emilio Nieves. We need more Emilios reaching the lost in the inner city, giving out clothes, and driving them to church.

•◆•

KEEP PLANTING SEEDS

If you speak with anyone who plants, farms, or gardens, they will tell you that it requires great patience to grow anything. Dealing with seeds is never a simple task. You have to find fertile ground, plant the seed, water the ground, wait for the seeds to break through the surface, and maintain the environment. It may take weeks, if not months, before you see any fruit from that seed. You have to consistently check on it.

This is exactly what Brother Emilio Nieves did for my family and me. He planted the seed of the gospel of Jesus, the gospel of hope. He didn't see immediate results, but he continued to come, honking his horn, inviting us to church with a smile, and blessing us with his generosity.

God's Word says, *"So let us not become tired of doing good; for if we do not give up, the time will come when we will reap the harvest"* (Gal. 6:9 GNB). Brother Emilio understood this principle very well. Today, I am a product of the seed he planted, and my entire family is blessed because he never stopped checking on the seeds he sowed.

Are you feeling discouraged because you've invested so much in others and haven't seen it pay off? Stay the course, and don't lose hope. It is a law of life that if you plant seeds, you will eventually reap a harvest. The key is to plant many seeds and not be stingy with them. I promise they will come back to you with bountiful dividends.

I leave you with these parting words: *"Remember that the person who sows few seeds will have a small crop; the one who sows many seeds will have a large crop"* (2 Cor. 9:6 GNB). Your job is to keep pouring into people, being a blessing to others. Brighten up someone's day, run an errand for them, and trust that God will reward you with an abundant harvest.

Keep planting seeds!

CHAPTER 14

◆

MARCOS RODRIGUEZ

I'm a firm believer that there are some people who come into your life for a season and for a reason. There are some people who, when they come into your life, just leave an imprint, and others simply leave. As I sit and write these lines, I can see that God was shaping my life every step of the way. Without a father or mother, God was shaping me into the man I am today.

If you get to know something about me, you would know that I have a great passion for the house of the Lord (the church). I have a special thing in me that lends itself to the important and significant details of the church. Are the rest rooms clean, is there enough toiletries, is the signage good, when are the cleaning crews scheduled, has the garbage been disposed of properly, and so forth . . . You just ask my team at the local church I pastor, and they will tell you.

As I think back, I have to say that a very important man in my life ingrained in me this mindset of caring for the house of God. His name is Marcos Rodriguez. Brother Marcos (who is now a pastor) was a local leader in our church. I can remember like it was today; he saw me at a midweek service and said, "Hey 'Pablito,' you want to hang out Saturday?" Starving for any affection I could get or hang out anywhere, I simply could not stand to be home with my grumpy grandma or stuck in the living room, so I said, "Yes, I would love that."

The first time Brother Marcos asked me, I remember when he picked me up in the church van. I was like, "Okay, we are hanging out in the church van," then he drove to our church on a late Saturday night and pulled out a big set of keys (big set of keys is an overstatement); anyone who knows Marcos Rodriguez knows he always had like 200 keys hanging from his side on his belt. As he opened the church, he swung the doors open to the empty church and said, "Okay, go into the closet, get a bucket, and fill it up with hot water; the mop is also in the closet, and you will begin by mopping the fellowship hall."

I was like, "Wait, what?" But I did it with no questions asked.

While I was mopping, he would just disappear, and I would hear him hammering or fixing things around the building. When I was done, I would advise him that I finished, then he would say, "Go upstairs and get the vacuum, get the long orange extension cord, attach it to the vacuum, and go around all the aisles of the church (three aisles of benches) and vacuum the sanctuary.

I was like, "Wait, what? I thought we were hanging out?" But, I did it.

Again, he would disappear, and when I was finished, I would go to him, and he would say, "Let's get a water hose and connect it to the outside on the side of the building and begin to wash away any dirt or debris in front of the church."

I was like (you already know) . . . "Wait, what?"

This was just on the first day of us "hanging out." We would do this routine week after week. By then, I began to love doing this. I felt like I knew that church building from the inside out, and I would brag to other youth I knew that I had the keys for closets, basements, and secret compartments.

As we cleaned week after week, I would put on music through the church sound system and worship while I mopped the fellowship hall. I learned how to reflect, meditate, and think while I was vacuuming the floor of the sanctuary. I learned to softly pray and intercede while I was out front spraying the concrete with water. I took great joy in cleaning the house of God because it was my time with him.

What I didn't know was that the Lord used Brother Marcos Rodriguez to instill this great value in me to have a love for the house of God. While my mother and father were somewhere getting high and nowhere to be found, while my brother and sister were home with my grandmother, and while all my friends were probably hanging out on a Saturday, God was shaping and molding me to care for his house.

Marcos Rodriguez is another mentor in my life. He never missed a day of service. He was the fix-it man in the church; he loved the house of the Lord, and now when I think back, I can't believe I, too, have 200 sets of keys. Hey, I may not have had a dad to show me how to fix cars or ask me to get him tools while he built something, but I had Marcos Rodriguez to show me how to work with excellence in the house of God. Truly, the scripture is fulfilled when it says God would be the father to the fatherless.

Today, I have to see the church I lead clean and smelling good. I ask my team to kindly have the best-smelling candles, get the best cleaning crew, and set teams to make sure the house of God is in order.

To all those reading this, you never know how you can be a Brother Marcos Rodriguez in someone's life. Being in church every Saturday night while everyone was probably hanging out saved my life, which kept me out of the corners of the ghetto; that gave me something to do and be proud of it, but above all, it helped me grow in my walk with Christ. I'm thankful that Marcos Rodriguez didn't volunteer me; he "voluntold" me.

MARCOS RODRIGUEZ

◆

TRUST THE PROCESS

If you were born or raised in the eighties, you might be familiar with a well-known movie that was so good they had to make it a trilogy. This movie is *The Karate Kid*. I absolutely loved this movie because it showcased the importance of tenacity and never giving up, even when life seems to be against you.

In one particular scene, a young boy named Daniel Larusso moves from Newark, New Jersey, to California and faces intense bullying. It is only when he seeks help from an older and wiser karate sensei named Mr. Miyagi that he begins to find a way to defend himself.

After pleading with Mr. Miyagi to train him, he is told to meet him at his house for training sessions. However, instead of receiving direct training, Daniel is given chores to do. He is told to wax Mr. Miyagi's car and paint his fence, and during these tasks, Mr. Miyagi repeats the phrases "wax on, wax off" and "paint up and paint down." Daniel becomes frustrated and exclaims, "I didn't come here to do your chores! I came to learn how to fight and defend myself."

What Daniel didn't realize is that these seemingly mundane tasks were actually part of his training. The movements he learned while waxing on and off and painting up and down became the foundation for his defense techniques when facing his bullies.

In my own life, I also encountered a Mr. Miyagi-like figure named Marcos Rodriguez. He was a leader at the church I attended and was responsible for cleaning the church. He would often invite me to help him, and even though I sometimes felt like I was being used as a servant, I would go because it allowed me to escape my home. Little did I know that God was using Marcos to shape me for my future. Anyone who knows me can attest that as a pastor, I have a deep appreciation for a clean and well-maintained church facility. It has become one of my greatest pet peeves. This is because my personal Mr. Miyagi, Marcos Rodriguez, instilled in me a love for the house of God.

You may find what you are currently learning or being forced to do annoying, but remember that the Bible says, *"You teach (train) my hands to fight and my arms to use a bow of bronze"* (Ps. 18:34 CEV). In other words, what you are doing today is preparing you for tomorrow.

I leave you with these parting words: We need more Marcos Rodriguez-type figures to help train young men for the battles they will face. Show them the ropes, teach them how to change a tire, check the oil, and even use a roller brush. You'll be surprised how these skills will come in handy when needed. So, young men, don't shy away from hard work early on because later in life, you will become a master craftsman in what you do.

◆

BECOMING PASTOR PABLO

◆

"Believe in the Lord Jesus and you will be
saved, along with everyone in your household"
(Acts 16:31 NLT).

CHAPTER 15

•◆•

MY PASTOR:
REV. RICARDO GUZMAN

My father always prayed for my mother, and he taught me never to despise her. I have to admit it was hard. I was so disappointed in her. I couldn't believe she left us again. Years went by. We continued to go to church as a family, and my father decided to join a church that would forever change the course of my life.

I feel that it's important for me to insert and dedicate a portion of this book to a church that played a huge role in my life, not just a church but its wonderful lead pastor. That church was Jehovah Shalom, and that pastor was Rev. Ricardo Guzman.

This pastor was a marvelous man. He received my family, heard our story, and ministered to us in every way possible. I remember how Pastor Guzman would call me after I would come out of school, and he would ask me to come to his office. Our church was a former movie theater, and his office was all the way at the top where the movie reels used to be played. I would go to his office upon his request, and he would simply call me there only to let me observe him take and make calls, conduct meetings, and study for teachings and sermon prep. I would

wonder why I was here after school. I would observe him advocate for the community as he would make calls to several elected officials.

On one occasion, I remember him teaching me about sermon preparation. I was only fourteen. He said to me, "You know, heaven is filled with messages. As a preacher, you never have to recycle a sermon or copy from someone else. Just keep your ears tuned to God, and He will give you a word."

One day, Pastor Guzman requested that I start giving the introduction to Sunday school classes. I was just opening up, but in order to do this, I had to be part of the Christian Education Committee and would have to come early to the teacher's class every Sunday morning. I did this for several months, and I enjoyed it. He must've seen something in me.

Soon, he asked that I be his everyday Sunday translator. Again, I was only fourteen; however, God didn't look at the age or qualifications. I would translate with the same passion he would preach, and soon, people were inviting me to translate their sermons and preach at their churches. My pastor always let me go as long I was at the church on my post every weekend.

I have so many fond moments of my dear pastor, a man who showed me the power of effective prayer and showed me to organize and rally people together for one common cause. Rev. Ricardo Guzman was a man who had vision and could see when God's hand and call was on someone. This was the man who was there for me in the most painful moment of my life.

THE APPRENTICE

N o, this devotional is not about President Donald Trump's former hit show on NBC called *The Apprentice*. However, I believe we can still glean and learn from this word today.

The word *apprentice* is defined as someone who is learning a trade, art, or calling through practical experience under skilled workers (Merriam Webster Dictionary).

Isn't that interesting? It simply means that we are learners. From the moment we are born, we are constantly adapting and learning. The truth is we learn from everything and everyone. We were created to absorb knowledge, like sponges. For example, you go to school and hear a friend say a curse word. You think nothing of it, but then you go home, and right in front of your parents, you blurt out your new vocabulary word (the curse word). What is their response? "Where did you learn that from?" or "Who taught you that word?" In your innocence, you are shocked by their reaction, thinking, "What did I do?"

Well, that day, you learned two things, maybe more:

Don't repeat everything your friends say.

Your parents just taught you about foul language (that was the day you learned about it).

You see, every experience and moment in life is a learning experience. To become an expert at something, you first have to be a good student or apprentice. God's Word says, *"Teach children how they should live, and they will remember it all their lives"* (Prov. 22:6).

In my case, I was an apprentice to my pastor at the time, and I didn't even know it. I watched him write sermons, handle phone calls, advocate for people, and run meetings, among other things. I was just there, minding my own business, not realizing I was an apprentice under a skilled man of God. I was being shaped for who I am today.

I leave you with these parting words: *"I have taught you wisdom and the right way to live. Nothing will stand in your way if you walk wisely, and you will not stumble when you run"* (Prov. 4:11–12 GNB).

Everything we do in life is orchestrated by God. He is filled with infinite wisdom and is ready to teach us. All we have to do is be willing to be His apprentice! Never stop learning.

◆◆◆

CHAPTER 16

THE DEATH OF MY FATHER

On May 1, 1998, I rose up early in the morning, and in my living room, there was my father on his knees, praying as he did each and every day. I heard him saying, "God, I ask you to cover my children, help them, and provide for them." He referred to me as Junior (since I'm named after him). He said, "Lord, guide Junior and fulfill your promises in him."

I left the house that morning and would never hear him again. When I returned home that afternoon, I recall hearing a message my older sister Brenda left on the answering machine. She said, "Junior, we've been trying to get ahold of you all day. When you get this message, please contact us. Dad went in for an appointment to the doctor, and he passed out at the hospital. Get here quick." I gathered my little brother and went to the hospital.

When I got to Jacobi Medical Center, my sister was there, and there were people from our church. A doctor walked up to my sister and me and asked her, "Are these your brothers?"

She said, "Yes, they are both here."

He looked at me and said, "We are sorry. Your dad did not make it. He had heart failure, and we couldn't bring him back. He was diagnosed with an enlarged heart." I just stood staring at the doctor as he continued, "You can go to the room and see the body."

As I went into the room, I saw my dear father with a tube sticking out of his mouth. It really looked like my dad was sleeping with his mouth open. I broke down in tears and began to slap him gently on the face, saying, "Get up, get up. Please, get up."

I suddenly felt a hand on my shoulder and heard a voice say, "Okay, it's time to come with me." The first person to console me at that moment was my pastor, Rev. Ricardo Guzman.

You know what amazes me until this day? My entire church leadership was in that hospital lobby. I haven't forgotten that.

I was seventeen years of age, and here we went again. I was an orphan; no dad or mom again! The story of my life! My mom was not around. She was missing and strung out. By this time, my grandmother had passed, so where would we go now?

For the next few days, my sweet, dear pastor, Rev. Ricardo Guzman, embodied what it was to comfort the broken. I recall one instance where he picked me up in his green conversion van. He drove to where we lived and told me to take him to the *bodega* (corner store), so I did. I'll never forget this. He went inside and asked the man, "How much money does the Pizarro family owe?" The man gave him the amount. He pulled out money, paid the owner of the store, and proceeded to tell him that my dad had passed away.

Growing up, the way my dad could do food shopping or buy anything for us was by getting a line of credit at the local store. He would send us to the store to buy essentials like bread, milk, rice (I would sneak in chips), and soap. Then, the store attendant would pull out a notebook, write my father's name down and the amount owed for that transaction, and at the end of the month, my father would pay for it. I believe my pastor knew that my dad didn't get to pay the end of April's bill, so he went and took care of my father's debt.

My father wasn't a rich man. He didn't leave us a will or money; however, my dad left me his remarkable faith. His funeral expenses were paid in full, and he had a nice funeral. God placed two outstanding individuals in my life who would help cover my father's entire funeral cost. Those two men were my employers and friends, Anthony Ocasio and Israel Peña. I recall as if it were today how they looked at me and said, "Don't worry. Everything will be taken care of." They walked into the funeral director's office and began to shell out hundred-dollar bills, paying for everything in cash.

When I come to think about it now, my father's last prayer on the last morning I would ever hear his voice was, "God, provide for my family and guide Junior." It's amazing because those very same guys who paid my father's funeral immediately took me in and let me live with them at seventeen years of age. My brother and my sister both moved in with my pastor, Rev. Ricardo Guzman (what a great man).

You might ask, "Why didn't you move in with your siblings and the pastor?" Let's just say that I already had plans. I met a young lady named Erika, and I had every intention of marrying her. As a matter of fact, I married her two months after my father's death, which was exactly a month before my eighteenth birthday. However, if you want to know about the love of my life, Erika, you'll have to wait and read the next book! I'll tell you everything about it there. Yup, I was married at seventeen years of age.

DEVOTIONAL

•◆•

BEING ABANDONED

Have you ever come across those viral videos on social media that depict animals being abandoned? I remember watching one about a dog from Texas. The owner placed the dog in the back of her car, and like any excited dog, he jumped in. The owner then drove to an empty lot, had the dog come out of the back seat, and simply left him in the middle of the street before driving away. The dog stood there with its ears drooped and its tail down, just staring as the car disappeared.

I couldn't help but wonder what was going through the dog's mind. How did this tragic moment shape his week, month, or even years? Did the dog cry that night? Did he struggle to sleep well during the first week? Did he wander for miles and miles, searching for his owner? Did that dog ultimately perish in his quest to find his owner? We may never know.

That is what abandonment looks like. It's someone walking out of your life or having them walk out on you without any explanations, leaving you with countless questions, emptiness, and pain.

When my father passed away, I questioned why God had to take him after he had turned his life around. Why now? I needed my father when I was a child, and I would have certainly needed him as a teenager and an adult. Why did he have to leave me? I felt so abandoned, searching for answers that seemed out of reach. It was the most intense pain I had ever experienced.

I felt like that dog left alone in the middle of the street, wondering where he had gone and why he left. God's Word says, *"Even if my father and mother abandon me, the Lord will take care of me"* (Ps. 27:10 CEV).

You may feel abandoned by the most important person in your life:

- Your husband may have walked out on you and the kids for another woman.
- Your father or mother may have run away from their responsibilities of raising you.
- Your children may have run away and left you.

Remember, God's promise is that He will take care of you.

I leave you with these parting words: *"For you will not abandon my soul to Sheol, or let your holy one see corruption"* (Ps. 16:10 CEB).

God has got you! You are not abandoned, but rather, you have been adopted.

CHAPTER 17

◆

TURNING MY BACK ON GOD

Losing my father was the most painful experience in my life. However, I've learned that life doesn't stop and wait for us. It keeps moving, so I simply tried keeping up with life. Here I was, a young man who had longed for his mom and dad's affection all his life and never really had it. Now, I was about to quickly enter adult life. By the time I turned eighteen, I was already going be a father.

Remember that prayer I made when I was eight years old? It was like God answered it slowly and in segments. He answered it piece by piece, like a puzzle during a span of years:

- He spared our family from going to a foster home.
- He healed my brother from being mute.
- He saved my father, who passed away as a believer.
- He guided me and protected me; he kept me grounded.

There was one big piece of the puzzle left. I had asked God to save both my mother and father, but as far as I remember, my mother was still given to her lifestyle of drugs.

Here I was now, a man eighteen years young, much more bitter and angry because for half my life, I had been abandoned and an orphan. Now, I was cluelessly married with one child. What I'll discuss here will be in my next book because I desire to share with you about the lessons of marriage and family life at a young age, along with all the lifetime of baggage we both brought into the relationship.

By the year 2000, my father had been deceased for two years, and I was a twenty-year-old young man who would soon be a father for the second time. I was on a lifelong journey searching for answers. My mother was in prison (again). I moved from New York City to New Jersey with the purpose of running from it all. I was deeply hurt with the passing of my father. I was angry at my mother. My brother and sister were living with my pastor. I was a father of two and already having marital issues with my wife. It seemed like the vicious cycle of family dysfunction was chasing after me.

During this time, I completely stopped going to church. All those experiences of cleaning the house of God, spending time with him, preaching in other churches, and going to prisons and telling people about what God did in my father was a mere memory. I was angry because I thought that God didn't answer the eight-year-old boy's prayer. I felt like he got it half right, and just when I started loving life and my dear dad, here came God and took him away. (At least those were my thoughts.)

I started to live a life I swore I would never live. I was always angry and upset. I thought that being abusive the way my father was before he became a Christian was the way to be. I also thought maybe I should drink to numb the anger and pain.

One day, I was so angry that I just went out and planned on getting so drunk, which I started to, and I picked up my little brother just to spend time with him. When I was going to take him back home, I got lost. At the time, I didn't know much about New Jersey. I was lost, drunk, and frustrated.

While trying to find my way back to take my brother, I saw an Assembly of God church, and I immediately stopped and just started crying. It was a Saturday night, I tried opening that church door, but it was locked. As I was going back into my car, I heard someone say, "Yes, can I help you?" I said to the man who came out, "Do you have service today?" He said, "No, we are just cleaning the temple," and he pointed inside. I said, "Okay, thanks," and this man (who I found out later was the pastor) said to me, "I don't know you, but God wants me to tell you that you belong on that pulpit (the stage or platform of the church)." He said, "You are running from everyone, and you're running from God because you lost your father."

Whatever I was drinking that day completely left me. I began weeping and knew that God's calling on my life was still there. The next day, Sunday, I attended the service with my wife and kids. I recommitted my life to Christ, and everything just got better!

Wait, but there's more. You guys remember my mother, right? At this point, she was still in prison in New York. She had no relationship with my kids or my wife, and somehow, out of the blue, she called me and said, "They will be releasing me from jail soon, and I have no family in New York. You guys all moved to New Jersey."

Do you know what I did? I hung up the phone! My wife immediately scolded me and said, "That's not nice. What happened to being Christlike and forgiving?" I have to admit that after hearing my wife tell me that, I felt very bad.

About a week later, my mother called again and said the same thing, but this time, I gave it thought. My mom asked if she could stay with me, and I very sternly told her, "You were never in my life, and now you want me to help you? Okay, I'll do it, but this house is my house, and you will respect, you will go to church, you will do as I say, you will not show my children the nonsense you did to us while growing up, and finally, you can't stay too long."

The time came when she was released, and she came to live with us. I didn't waste time. I was mean, belligerent, and rude.

One Sunday morning, I told her to get up; it was time to go to church because in this house, we went to church. She outright told me, "I'm not going." I was livid and got nasty with her. Something told me, "Cool off and just ask her why she puts you and your family through everything she put you guys through. Speak to her. Ask her why she does this." When I did, she simply began to cry and told me, "I was raped by my own father. When I told my mother, she didn't believe me. They put me in a foster home till I was seventeen. I met a man who I was not married to, and he said he would return after he went to serve as a Merchant Marine, but he never came back for me." Then, she met my father, who apparently was the love of her life, but if you've been reading so far, you know how that turned out.

The love of her life (my father) beat her and abused her, never honored her, and married her after being with her for eighteen years, and to top it off, she miscarried and lost thirteen babies. When she did have kids, her eldest was born addicted to crack and cocaine, and the youngest was born premature and addicted to crack and cocaine.

When it comes to me, people ask, "Well, what happened with you?" Well, my mother explained to me that while she was pregnant with me, she was incarcerated for nine months. She was clean, and when she came out, she gave birth to me. This is why I know that God had separated me from my mother's womb. My favorite verse is Jeremiah 1:5, "I knew you before I formed you in your mother's womb. Before you were born I set you apart and appointed you as my prophet to the nations."

After hearing my mom explain all this to me about the abuse in her life and how her father failed her, her first husband failed her marriage, and then my father failed her, I felt God say: "Don't be the next man to fail her." It was from that day on that I started loving my mom. Just by loving her and helping her get back on her feet, she started coming around, helping to take care of my kids, getting along with my wife, and one day, on her own, she got up and went to church. Guess what? She gave her heart to the Lord and never left.

We moved to Jersey and she has been clean 21 years, and now I have the greatest honor of being her pastor. She's been the perfect grandmother. She's done things for my two kids that she never ever did for my siblings or me. She's lived and put her second chance in life as a grandmother. Whatever she didn't get right in the first half of her life, she sure has made up for it.

Oh, and by the way, God fulfilled the prayer of an eight-year old boy because he saved my mother, father, and both my brother and sister are all serving the Lord with me in Newark, New Jersey.

So, I kept my end of the prayer, and I'm telling you about how good God is.

DEVOTIONAL

◆

TURNING HEEL

"Turning heel" refers to a player or person shifting from a "face" persona to a "heel" persona, transitioning from a "good guy" to a "bad guy." I learned this term from wrestling and sci-fi movies.

One of the most notable examples of someone "turning heel" is when Hulk Hogan was reintroduced as "Hollywood Hogan" and joined the New World Order (NWO). It was unimaginable to witness Hulk Hogan, whom we had always seen defending the innocent and doing what was right, transform into an evil villain.

As incredible as it may seem, sometimes the enemy of our souls, referred to as the devil in the Bible, convinces us to turn heel on our Lord and Savior, Jesus Christ. The devil also tries to turn us against those who love us the most, including God, just as Hulk Hogan did.

The devil whispers lies and doubts into our ears, persuading us that we don't need God, that we can handle everything on our own. Gradually, without even realizing it, we start to distance ourselves from God, turning our backs on His love and grace.

I vividly remember the moment it happened to me. It was a dark and lonely time in my life, filled with pain and confusion. I had always been a faithful follower of Christ, regularly attending church and praying, but the enemy saw an opening, a crack in my armor, and he seized the opportunity.

He whispered doubts about my worthiness, purpose, and faith. He made me question everything I had once believed in. And in that moment of weakness, I made the choice to turn my back on God. I abandoned my faith, rejecting His love and guidance.

It was a gradual process, like a slow descent into darkness. I stopped going to church, ceased praying, and no longer sought God's will in my life. Instead, I embraced a life of selfishness and sin, indulging in worldly pleasures and seeking fulfillment in all the wrong places.

But just like Hulk Hogan eventually realized the error of his ways and turned face again, finding redemption in the wrestling ring, I, too, reached a breaking point. The emptiness and guilt became unbearable, and I longed for the peace and joy that only God can provide.

In that moment of desperation, I fell to my knees and cried out to God. I confessed my sins, my doubts, and my rebellion. And in His infinite mercy, He welcomed me back with open arms. He forgave me and restored my faith, reminding me that His love is unconditional, and His grace is sufficient.

Turning my back on God was the biggest mistake of my life, but it also became the catalyst for my spiritual growth and transformation. Through the pain and consequences of my actions, I learned the importance of staying rooted in God's truth and relying on His strength.

Now, I strive to live a life that reflects God's love and grace. I aim to be a light in the darkness, sharing the message of redemption and hope with others who may have also turned their backs on God. I know firsthand the power of His forgiveness and the joy of being reconciled to Him.

If you find yourself at a crossroads, tempted to turn your back on God, remember that He is always waiting with open arms. No matter how far you've strayed or how deep you've fallen, His love and grace are greater than any mistake or rebellion. Turn back to Him, and you will find forgiveness, restoration, and a love that will never let you go.

"They would have been better off if they had never known about the right way. Even after they knew what was right, they turned their backs on the holy commandments they were given. What happened to them is just like the true saying, 'A dog will come back to lick up its own vomit. A pig that has been washed will roll in the mud'"

(2 Pet. 2:21–22 CEV).

DEL
ARDIENTE FUEGO
AL
PARAISO